SCHMOOPIE'S DREAM
From *Pound to Penthouse*

SCHMOOPIE'S DREAM

From Pound to Penthouse

Patricia Garfield

Tiburon, California, USA

Schmoopie's Dream: From Pound to Penthouse
Copyright © 2014, Patricia Garfield, Ph.D.
All rights reserved. Printed in the United States of America.
No part of this book may be used or reproduced in any
manner without prior written permission, except in the case
of brief quotations embodied in critical articles and reviews.

Photo credit: Richard Wilkerson
  for Portrait of Patricia Garfield
Photos of Schmoopie: by members of her
  human family
Cover & Interior design: JM Shubin, BookAlchemist.net

CATALOGING DATA:
  Schmoopie's dream: from pound to penthouse
  Patricia Garfield, Ph.D.
  Children's

ISBN: 978-0-9916174-1-8

Contents

1.	Alone	9
2.	Visiting Day	13
3.	White, White	19
4.	The Door	23
5.	Afloat	29
6.	Airborne	35
7.	Elevator Guard	41
8.	Cross Country Westward	47
9.	Hollywood Dog Star Hotel	53
10.	Cross Country Eastward	63
11.	Homecoming	67
12.	Afterword	79
	Listen Up!	85

A Short List of Good Films Featuring Dogs
A Few Facts about the Dog Star
A Few Facts about Dogs

About the Author	97

For the family members of Schmoopie's Den,
especially the two youngest additions,
George and Anderson.
With love.

Chapter 1

Alone

I was alone. Cold ... so cold.

There had been others. Although my eyes were still sealed shut, their warm fur snuggled against my sides had been a comfort. Their whimpering as they nuzzled, groping for milk, had been my lullaby.

Mama's rough tongue licked me to sleep.

But one by one, the others grew chilly against me and fell silent.

My crusted eyes struggled open ...

"Hey, Mac, this one's alive!"

"Phew! What a runt – nobody will buy that

SCHMOOPIE'S DREAM

mutt. And it's got a weird mark on its forehead. Get rid of it, Joe. Take it to the dump."

A big creature with head fur scooped me up in a dirty towel and tossed me into a cardboard box on the front seat of his truck.

Oof! What's happening?

Joe swung into the driver's seat, revved the engine, and threw the truck into gear. He tucked the towel closer to ease my shivering.

I licked his hand. He tasted salty. Smelled of oil and mustard.

"A pity," Joe murmured. "You're a sweet pup. The color of honey – might make some kid happy." He scratched the dark diamond between my eyes where Mama used to lick. "But no room in my house."

He pulled out of the garage and headed toward the dump.

Rumbling along the freeway, a thought jiggled loose. Joe mumbled aloud, "It'll only take a minute. Give the runt a chance. Mac will never know. Or care." He swung off the ramp, pulled

ALONE

up and parked in front of the big brick building of the Humane Society.

Joe lifted the cardboard box and carried it in to the counter. A chat with the bright-eyed brunette receptionist, a bit of paperwork, and he was on his way home to early dinner.

"Good luck, kiddo," he called.

What is going on? No! He's leaving me, too! Help!

Alone again. A cold cage. A kennel. Not even a dirty towel for warmth.

The bright-eyed lady held a bottle of warm milk to my lips for a few minutes. She left a bowl of cool water in the cage, some mushy stuff in a dish, and a rubber-thing to chew on. It smelled of dozens of dogs. Smelled a little like hope.

Yawn. So tired ...

I kneaded the air with my paws.

I sucked.

My closed eyes darted back and forth.

My tail flip-flopped. Little whistles puffed my lips. They were back beside me – all my brothers and sisters, nestled close. Warm. Cozy.

11

Schmoopie's Dream

Pop! The dream vanished. My eyes snapped open. I stared into darkness. Chilly metal mesh surrounded me. No one.

Loneliness swept over me like a tossed pail of water.

I set my head down on my paws and whimpered.

A baby. Alone.

Chapter 2

Visiting Day

"Looking good, little girl." Bright Eyes gave me an affectionate pat.

I felt good, too. My coat had been bathed, dried and brushed. Healthy food and kind care for two weeks had helped. I was not so scrawny. I could see without those crusts on my eyes and I have stopped shivering all the time. *This place is not so bad.*

Bright Eyes checked my ears and eyes.

"Nice and clear. All set to meet the public! Might be your lucky day."

SCHMOOPIE'S DREAM

In the visiting room, my cage was set midway down the line. Dogs big and small, in nearby cages, displayed themselves to advantage.

The regal Great Dane stood taller when the first visitors climbed the steps to the pound. The Poodle with papers stepped daintily around her cage as if at a dog show where she knew she would win the blue ribbon. A golden Cocker Spaniel tilted its ears from one side to the other, flirting. A yappy Chihuahua challenged all comers. Several purebloods...and a few mixed breeds. Their scents filled the air.

Who would choose me? *A runt.* I laid my head on my well-brushed paws and gazed sadly at the "superior beings" exhibited on either side of me.

The front door swung open. Early visitors poured into the pound. Kids ran back and forth beside the line of cages in excitement.

A boy sucking a lollypop raced along the metal cages, rattling each one. I shrank from his sticky finger.

A girl in a plaid dress reached over and tugged my tail. *Ye-Ouch!*

VISITING DAY

A heavy-set man said to everyone in general, "We want a sturdy guard dog!"

Whoosh! The door flung open again. Terrified, I braced against the next attack.

And there she stood. Tall. Slender. Long light hair. Sunlight behind her made her silhouette glow.

My mistress! I *knew.* I felt it in my fragile bones. I lifted my head, perked up my ears, and gazed in awe at the figure wearing a soft blue running suit and blue shoes.

Please, please, see me. Like me!

The slender young woman and her mate, an Alpha Male, it was clear from his sturdy stance, strolled alongside the display cages. They stopped at the end and turned. Pacing slowly back, they studied the faces and postures of each pooch.

The couple paused briefly at my cage. Did I imagine Mistress squeezing the man's arm? My heart raced. But they walked back to the start of the line.

The man shrugged his shoulders, pointed at

SCHMOOPIE'S DREAM

me and said. "I like that one."

I shook. Bright Eyes came over, unclipped the cage door and lifted me out. I was shaking when she placed me in Mistress's arms. Delicious scents filled my nostrils, vanilla and citrus fruit.

Mistress fastened her eyes, blue as the sky, on mine. Maybe *she* knew, too.

"What lovely warm brown eyes she has – just like my father's! And look at her velvety diamond." With a long forefinger, Mistress stroked the spot that Mama used to lick. I trembled. "Oh, yes, let's take her." Mistress handed me to the man.

"Done!" said my new Master, handing me back after a quick inspection.

"She's only six weeks old," Bright Eyes said. "Almost too young to adopt. She never had a home. She came to us as a newborn, her eyes half-open. A runt. But she's a survivor and quickly grew stronger. You'll need to train her gently."

"What kind of pup is she?" asked Mistress.

"A mutt – probably a mix of Shepherd and

Visiting Day

Collie. It's hard to be sure this young."

Arrangements made, Mistress cradled me carefully. I quivered. They took me home for the trial period.

Will they keep me? Will I have a real home? Her face is kind ...

Chapter 3
White, White

"Here we are, little Schmoopie. This is your new home." Sean, our driver, stopped the Town Car in front of a tall building with a green awning and glass doors.

Mistress kept calling me "Schmoopie." *Funny name.* I laid my ears back and stared. A big man in a red uniform with shiny buttons stood in front.

"Say hello to Brian," Mistress said to me. "He's our doorman."

Master carried a large box from a store he and Mistress stopped at on our way here. Brian held the door wide open to let us enter.

SCHMOOPIE'S DREAM

"Good afternoon, Sir."
"How's it going, Brian?"
"Hunky-dory so far, Sir."
"Keep it that way."
We crossed the lobby to a small brass room with lots more buttons. Mistress pressed one marked "P." A motor purred. The small room shut one side and jiggled for a few seconds, smoothing to a stop.

We got out and, with a key, Mistress opened yet another door and held it while Master hefted the big box inside.

White! Everything inside the room was white. White walls, white carpets, white chairs. Mistress set me down gently. I sank. The carpet was so cushy I couldn't balance. I wobbled.

Too much space. Too white. Too bright. I scrambled across the dense whiteness as if climbing across the back of a thick-furred poodle. I hustled as fast as I could behind the white couch. *Quick. Into the dark. Hide.* I cringed, out of the reach of groping hands.

"Schmoopie, Schmoopie. Come out, come

White, White

out, wherever you are," Mistress coaxed.

I whimpered and crouched lower.

"Leave her be for a while. Let her get used to it," said Master to Mistress.

They left the room. I heard dishes clink against silverware. Delicious odors drifted under the couch. I licked my lips but didn't move. I fell asleep for a while.

I awoke to loud scratching sounds as the couch slid away from the wall. Mistress scooped me out of the snug dark corner. I squirmed. *No! No! Too much space. Scary.*

"Come along, Schmoopie dear. Test your new bed." Mistress carried me, wriggling, to her dressing room where she set me into a cushion-padded basket. "Feel how comfy."

Mistress slid the basket against the back wall. Above my head hung shirts that smelled like Mistress. Sweet, fruity, vanilla-y. Many were blue as the sky, like her eyes. She shut the closet doors partway. "Come out when you're ready," she said.

I lay in the semi-dark with cushions cozy

21

Schmoopie's Dream

beneath me. I didn't move. I was safe.

Gurgling in my tummy got louder. Yummy odors from the kitchen tickled my nostrils. I peeked out of the crack between the doors. Inhaled deeply, and ventured into the squishy white vastness.

"There you are!" Mistress sat alone in the kitchen. "Look, Schmoopie. This is your water bowl. Here is your lunch."

I daintily nosed the mush, took a tentative mouthful and lapped some water.

Master strode into the kitchen. His heavy step on the white tile floor terrified me again. I peed.

Oh, no! I scrambled, tried to run. My claws scratched and slid on the tile. Mistress scooped me up. Paper towels floated down like large snowflakes. Mistress gingerly carried me back to the basket.

"*Shh! Shh!* It's O.K. You just need a little time. You're safe here." She set me back in the cozy closet bed. Worn out once more, I slept.

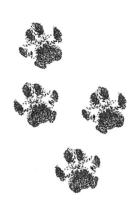

Chapter 4
The Door

```
Six Months Later
```

I woke, stretched, and trotted out of my closet-bed with a sure step. *Time to check on Mistress.*

Morning was my favorite time of day. Master was at his office. I had Mistress's full attention.

"Good morning, Schmoopie!" Mistress greeted me. She rubbed my ears until I wriggle-danced. "Wait 'til you see your surprise today."

I loved Mistress's surprises. She made every day feel like a holiday with some new treat or adventure.

Best was our morning walk through the park across the street. Mistress attached a handsome

SCHMOOPIE'S DREAM

leather leash to my collar. We took the elevator to the lobby.

"G'morning Madame, Schmoopie." Brian held open the glass door and gave me a pat.

"Morning!" Mistress smiled.

"A bit nippy now, but warming."

I trotted briskly, setting a comfortable pace for Mistress to follow. I admit it, I'm proud of my long-legged Mistress in the plush-sky-blue running suit. Most things are shades of grey to my eyes, but blue shines. *My Lady is a purebred.*

We waited for the green light at the crosswalk. I sniffed the curb and newspaper stand to check the scents of recent visitors. The usual. No problem.

On the park side of the street, delicious odors floated everywhere. Spicy pine. Saucy hot dogs. Squirrels! Horses!! Each left a trail I could follow for hours. But my job was to lead Mistress safely.

I waited patiently when Mistress stooped to pick up a brightly colored fallen leaf or shapely twig to take home to sketch.

Oh, there's that pesky squirrel! He had come low

THE DOOR

enough on the trunk to be catchable. I strained at the leash.

"No, no, Schmoopie! Just watch. Don't chase."

Then came the joyous moment when Mistress unsnapped my leash. I dashed here and scampered there. I splashed at the edge of the fountain, sniffed the park benches, and nibbled a dropped bit of hot dog. Endless pleasures ...

After the park, the penthouse felt small. No longer too much, as I used to think. Not even enough space to run and bark, turn and wheel. Or sprint.

Something was different today. Mistress had arranged for workmen to come in while we were in the park. Martha, the daily maid, cleaned up bits of scraps and sawdust the workmen's broom had missed.

"Here it is, Madam, " said the workman in the plaid shirt. "Is this what you wanted?"

"Yes, it looks perfect! Thank you very much." She signed some papers. The two men tipped their caps and carried away toolboxes. Martha

SCHMOOPIE'S DREAM

set out lunch.

"Look, Schmoopie!" Mistress pointed. "Your new door."

I stared. The workmen had cut a small door into the wall next to the usual door to the terrace.

I waited. Wagging my tail, I looked at Mistress. *What does she want?*

"It's for you!" Mistress said. I raised my brow and ears.

Woof! *I'm glad she's happy, but what's the surprise?*

Mistress reached down and pushed the door with her hand. It swung.

I looked at the door, at Mistress's face, at the door again. I wagged. *What?*

Mistress frowned. *Uh-oh.* Mistress got down on her hands and knees until she was nose to nose with me. She turned to the small new door and crawled through.

Hide and Seek! I know that game. My back end boogied. *Arf!*

Mistress called, "Schmoopie, come here. Come!" I danced in a circle.

26

The Door

Mistress pushed the door partway open, still on her hands and knees. *Come!"*
I crept closer, crouched. Mistress beckoned. Slowly I crawled through to the other side. Outdoors!
"Yes! Yes, good dog."
But Mistress crawled back through. I was alone on the terrace. *Look! Birds over my head!*
"Come on, Schmoopie!" I stared at the small door and crept through again.
Oh! Wonderful! Back and forth, I raced. In and out. *By myself. No key needed.*
Good Mistress! I licked Mistress's face like my Mama used to lick mine, the best kind of doggie "thank you."
Back and forth I scampered. Inside. Outside. Inside. *My own door. Never locked. Fun!*
Arf! Arf!.

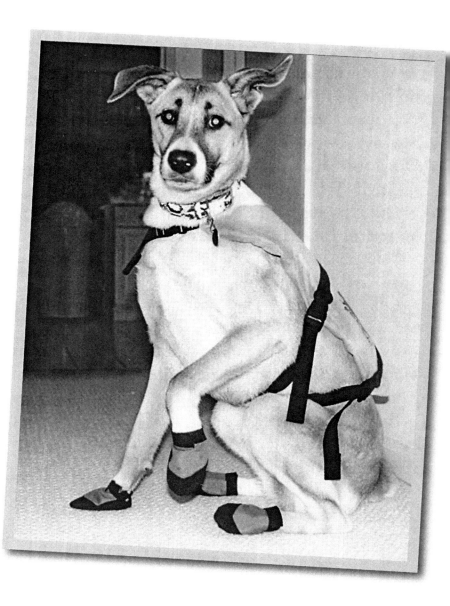

Chapter 5

Afloat

One Year Old

The sun sparkled through the kitchen windows. Spring clouds blew across the sky like dandelion puffs in the wind.

"Today you get your birthday treat, Schmoopie."

Although I had grown much bigger in the last year, Mistress still took me on her lap to cuddle. She rubbed my favorite spots. Behind my ears. Under my chin. The dark diamond between my eyes. I licked the tip of Mistress's nose.

What treat? I have nearly everything. I eyed my half-chewed squishy-squirrel toy. Not as good as catching the pesky squirrel in the park, but

SCHMOOPIE'S DREAM

almost. Especially when I shake it hard and bite it to make it squeal. *A new squishy?*

"You've learned so much. We think you're ready."

Ready for what? My ears perked up. I wagged my tail. Waited.

"You'll see. We need to go for a drive first."

I hopped down from Mistress's lap to fetch my leash.

The Town Car waited at the curb when Mistress came through the glass doors. Brian gave me my daily pat as we passed. Master already waited in the back seat.

Sean opened the car's backseat door, curbside. I leaped in and took the middle seat. Mistress followed.

"To the Harbor, Sean," said Master.

"Right you are, Sir."

Mistress adjusted my special motoring glasses: Doggles. They felt weird the first time Mistress strapped them on my face. I had tried to shake them off.

But now I loved them. Across Mistress's body,

30

AFLOAT

I hung my head out the side window. No danger of eye grit.

Sean steered our Town Car through crowded city streets. Wonderful new scents floated on the air – pizza from street carts, stray mutts nosing tipped trashcans. Lots to sniff and see in this part of town.

Sean skillfully swung the Town Car into a reserved parking slot in front of a large boat. Sleek. Elegant. A yacht. *I've seen those on television.*

Mistress took a package out of her tote bag and tore it open. "Schmoopie, dear, today you must wear booties. The deck's just been varnished. No scratches allowed."

I raised my brow and cocked my ears. *What are booties?*

Out of the package, Mistress pulled four suede pouches with drawstrings. She slid one bootie on each of my paws, drew the cords snugly, and tied them in place. I chewed at the last knot.

"No. No! Leave them be."

I stopped. I got out of the car at Mistress's command and heeled. One by one, Master,

31

SCHMOOPIE'S DREAM

Mistress, and I crossed a ramp onto the deck of the yacht. Sean stayed at the wharf and waved as the boat moved backward, turned, and traveled to the mouth of the harbor.

Whoa ... what's happening? The deck underfoot shook, tilted slightly. A motor purred. Strange vibrations crept up my legs. I braced myself, got tipped off balance, braced again.

"It's O.K.," Mistress said, giving me a reassuring pat. "You'll soon get used to it."

Mistress was right. There were marvelous scents on the sea breeze. A cafeteria of new bird and water smells. I ventured to the side of the deck and set my head on the railing. I faced my nose into the breeze and inhaled.

My paws felt cozy inside the soft suede. The Doogles kept my eyes clear. I watched people on other boats. Some vessels came in, others went out. *Like a park on water! And no leash needed!*

I sniffed, observed, sniffed more. Mistress tossed pieces of popcorn. I loved to catch and chew the white puffs. Master smiled, his arm around

32

Afloat

Mistress. Her light hair streamed behind her.

When we returned to port hours later, I spotted a dark figure near some crates. I caught his scent on the breeze. Something about that man ... My legs stiffened. The hair on my neck bristled. I laid back my ears. *Growl.* The throaty sound surprised me.

"It's all right," said Mistress. The figure vanished. But something was *not* all right. *What was it?*

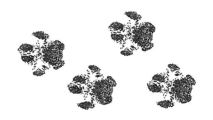

Chapter 6

Airborne

Three Months later

I stood with Mistress at the edge of a field full of odd objects. *What are they?* I licked Mistress's hand. *What?*

Sean had just driven Master, Mistress, and me to this place. But it was not the harbor and those things were not boats.

WHIRR! The sound of a giant vacuum cleaner hurt my eardrums. It grew louder. Startled, I looked up.

It's in the sky! A big bird with wings on its head. Danger! Danger! Arf, arf! I tugged hard at my leash. *Mistress, follow me to safety!*

SCHMOOPIE'S DREAM

"It's O.K., Schmoopie. I know it's noisy, but a helicopter ride is fun. You'll see." Mistress petted my back with long soothing strokes from my neck to the base of my spine. "Just wait 'til you see where we're going."

Strong wind buffeted my fur and blew my ears straight back. The huge metal bird screeched and lowered to earth as if settling on its nest. It stopped. Its mouth plopped open and an iron ladder dropped out.

"See you later, Sean." Master waved. He climbed the wobbly iron stairway with us trailing behind.

Mistress urged me up the steps. A man in overalls shoved my rump from behind. Master helped us enter. He took a seat.

Inside the belly of the Big Metal Bird, Mistress sat down and buckled her safety belt. I crouched on the rumbling floor, my head on her feet. The man in overalls pulled the ladder inside and secured the door. He sat at a wheel near a lot of dials.

"Long Island today," Master said to the pilot.

36

AIRBORNE

"Yes, sir. Looks like a clear flight. Everyone buckled in?"

Big Metal Bird screeched again and launched into the sky.

The floor rumbled louder beneath my paws. I laid back my ears, bared my teeth.

"Look out the window, Schmoopie!" Mistress said. She tapped her fingernail on the small oval window. I pressed my nose to the glass. "See our car way below? There's Sean waving."

Sean is shrinking! Buildings got smaller. Cars looked like toys. I raised my brows.

Higher and faster we rose. Shakier. I leapt off the floor onto Mistress's lap. I trembled all over. Mistress stroked my fur and cooed. "Mmm, hmm ... See our boat way over there on the water?"

Wisps of cloud floated by the window. Passing birds grew tiny below us. Cars the size of ants crawled on little paths. Swimming pools turned into birdbaths. On and on we flew ...

37

SCHMOOPIE'S DREAM

Big Metal Bird lowered down, down. Blue water stretched out with no end in sight. More water than any pond in Central Park. White birds swooped across the surface. They fluttered to a long strip of sand and lifted back into the air.

Houses grew larger. Trees got bigger. Metal Bird roared, landed, stopped its terrible noise and shaking. Its mouth-door opened. The stepladder dropped down like a hot tongue.

"Smooth landing! Good job," Master called to the pilot. He descended the iron stairs and reached up to help the rest of us down.

"That was your first helicopter ride, Schmoopie. You'll soon get used to it," he said.

Back on a surface that did not wobble, I stood still and gave my body a great shake. *Whew!*

The next few hours were filled with delicious adventures. First, we lunched in the snack bar at the small airport, cool water and kibble for me. A driver took us to our destination, the Beach House.

Soft sand squished under my paws. Water

AIRBORNE

moved in and out. Wave after wave crashed onto the sand and backed away, like a game of tag. I barked and raced to catch a wave. I snapped at it. *Bleeh! Salty! Achoo!* I shook my muzzle.

Seagulls dipped and rose above the surfaces of the waves. *Arf!* I dashed to chase them. Mistress never said, "No!"

I danced in the mild surf. The sun warmed my wet fur. Marvelous objects covered the beach. Odd shells. Crawling things. Half-buried mysteries with wonderful scents. Enough to keep any dog happy for hours.

When we went inside the Beach House to rest, I flopped on the soft matting. *So this is The Beach. Big Metal Bird flies us here in her belly.*

I slept blissfully. I dreamed of deer and geese invading the waving grass in front of the Beach House. I chased them with glee...until my old nightmare of cuddling with Mama Dog and all my siblings returned. *Where were they?* I woke in a startle.

"Come, Schmoopie, time to go home!" called Mistress.

39

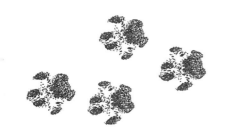

Chapter 7

Elevator Guard

"Hey Joe, I was down at the wharf yesterday picking up the new shipment of pups. Saw a strange thing."

"What's that, Mac?" Joe asked. He glanced at his boss from where he stooped hosing out cages for the new arrivals.

"Remember about a year ago when we got that bad shipment of pups that died?"

"Yeah?" A shiver ran up Joe's neck.

"There was one runt that survived? I told you to dump it ..."

"A lot of pups pass through here and get shipped out again in a year, Mac."

SCHMOOPIE'S DREAM

"This one had a weird mark on its forehead. Remember?"

"Nah, can't say I do." Joe busily scrubbed the cage floor with a steel brush.

"Well the thing is, I saw its grownup twin yesterday. Getting off a fancy yacht and into a Town Car. We could use a dog like that to breed. Tough. Strong."

"Forget it, Mac. Let sleeping dogs lie. It might bring cops sniffing around your business."

"Maybe, but I'm going to check it out next chance I have. Could triple our profit."

"Hmm ..." Joe had his head inside the next dirty cage.

I trotted ahead of Mistress on our morning run in Central Park. Leafy elm trees formed shady borders along our path. I sniffed for any dropped snacks among the newly opened narcissus. Pesky squirrels chattered, unfairly out-of-reach in branches, probably plotting to snatch food scraps before I could get them. Birds twittered. I never ran too far ahead. I paused to sniff fresh

ELEVATOR GUARD

scents on park benches, turned and waited, wagged my tail. *Mistress runs well but she only has two legs, so she's not as fast as I am. Too bad we can't race together.*

I felt frisky and fresh. I wanted to test my strength. At the end of the path rose a steep stone staircase. I glanced back. Mistress was trailing behind. I burst into a run. Up, up, up the stairway I flew. No holding back. Full speed. Up and over the crest.

What is taking my Lady so long? There's nothing to it. Go!

I felt as impatient as a jogger at a stoplight. *I know! I'll surprise her. She gives me lots of surprises. She thinks I don't know the way home. But I do. Three blocks East straight across the park. Turn left. Cross the street, then right into our apartment building. Brian will be waiting at the door.*

I sprinted off, as if in a race. *Quick, before Mistress reaches the top.*

"Hello there, Schmoopie," said Brian, holding open the door. "Where's your mistress?"

SCHMOOPIE'S DREAM

I wagged my tail in greeting. *Coming. She's coming.* I trotted to the open elevator, entered and faced front in a stance of power. I stood tall and strong, and gazed straight ahead. *Mistress will be shocked. I'm big enough now to help.*

The lobby clock tick-tocked. Mr. Olsen from floor twelve came through the glass doors with a bag of fresh strawberries for lunch. As he approached the elevator, I lowered my ears.

`Grr!` *It was a polite warning. This elevator is reserved for Mistress.*

Mr. Olsen backed away and looked around for Brian. Mrs. Oggleby from floor seven approached carrying three plastic bags covering freshly cleaned clothes. A delivery boy with a pizza box that sent out waves of warm-smelling tomato sauce and cheese hesitated.

`Grr!`

Brian picked up the telephone at the reception desk and punched a number.

"Sir, I know you're busy at the office, but Schmoopie's returned from the park without your

44

ELEVATOR GUARD

wife. She won't let anyone on the elevator. I think she's holding it for her."

My ears perked up.

"Yes, sir. Her cell phone? I don't have that number. You'll call? Thanks very much." Brian stepped over to the group gathering to board the elevators.

"Sorry to inconvenience you folks," he said. "There's been a mix-up. As you can see, the other elevator is being serviced." He pointed to the sign displayed beside it. "Please be patient. It'll only be a short wait."

A buzz of grumbling and chatter arose. I stood alert. On guard.

Whoosh! The lobby door flung open.

There she is at last! Mistress's face was flushed and her eyes bright. She was breathing fast. Tail awag, I pranced forward to greet her.

"Sorry everyone," Mistress said. "Thanks for calling about this, Brian."

People smiled, shrugged, sighed. I was now off guard duty. They boarded the elevator. Mr. Olson kept the elevator on hold while Mistress

45

Schmoopie's Dream

embraced me.

"Oh, Schmoopie." Mistress shook her head and hugged me again. "You're full of surprises these days. Come on, let's have lunch."

Chapter 8
Cross Country Westward

Our Den was buzzing with suitcases being packed and repacked. Mistress was leaving on a business trip to Hollywood for several weeks. She would not go without me, yet she did not want me to travel by cargo. Said I'd be too cold and hungry. The airline people ruled me too big to have a seat of my own in the plane. *What's their problem? I'm only 79 pounds.*

What to do? Master and Mistress had long discussions. The outcome was: I would ride across the entire country with Sean, our trusty driver, at the wheel. Master, as Pack Leader,

SCHMOOPIE'S DREAM

would stay home to guard the Den.

Suitcases, finally locked, stood ready by the door. Special supplies for the road and for use on the West Coast were stowed in the car or shipped. I've had my shots. I took an extra trip to the groomer's where they washed, dried, and brushed my thick coat until it gleamed. *Looks fabulous, if I say so myself. Strange to be leaving the Den.*

On departure day, Mistress held me close to give her instructions.

"This trip will be a big adventure for you, Schmoopie. You will see things you never saw before. Sean will send photos to me on this smart phone so I can see where you are. Every night I will speak with you over the telephone. We'll be back together in five days. You must be brave and good. I count on you."

I licked the tip of Mistress's nose to assure her not to worry. But I've never been away from the Master and Mistress since the day they brought me home from the pound. I'm uneasy, even with Sean beside me. *What if things go wrong?*

CROSS COUNTRY WESTWARD

"Take care of your Mistress," ordered Master. He patted me goodbye. Sean loaded everything into the Town Car. We would drop Mistress at the airport before driving directly onward across the country.

When Mistress said goodbye at the airport gates, I whined. *Will I see her again?*

"Remember what I said, Schmoopie. Love you." She gave me one last kiss between my brows where Mama used to lick. Then the airport crowd swallowed her.

Schmoopie's Dream

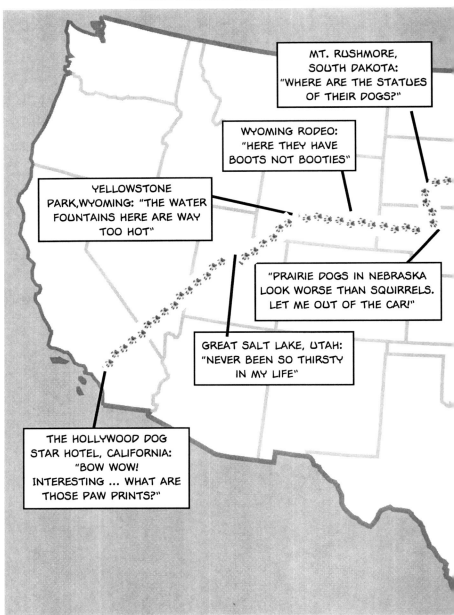

CROSS COUNTRY WESTWARD

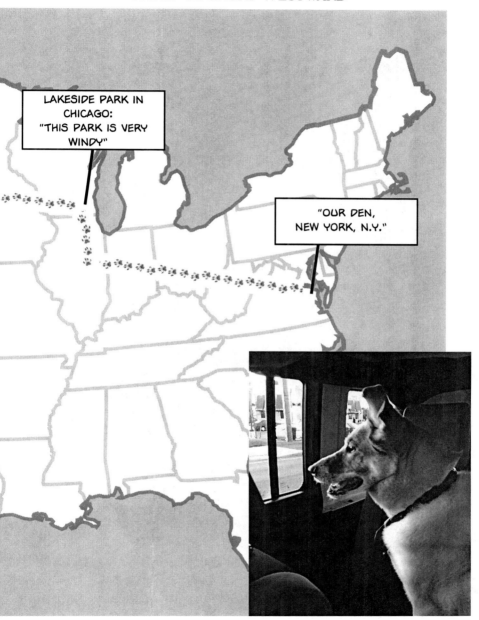

Chapter 9

Hollywood Dog Star Hotel

Sean eased our Town Car to a stop in front of the Hollywood Dog-Star Hotel. He hopped out and opened the car door for Mistress and me, now reunited on the West Coast.

We stood at the entrance to a posh-looking building. A dark blue awning shielded us from the Southern California sunshine. A red carpet spreading from the curb to hotel door cushioned my paws.

To either side of the padded walkway, pairs of dog-paw prints were preserved in the concrete sidewalk. Above each pair blazed a bronze star.

SCHMOOPIE'S DREAM

Mistress had been staying in one of this hotel's suites with special amenities for dogs who are movie stars (or hope to be). She pointed out the names written in the cement of the movie star dogs whose prints are honored.

"Those big prints are Rin Tin Tin's," she said. "Lassie made the slender pair over further." There are a dozen others.

Inside the lobby, the wall behind the check-in counter was covered with a panel of blue-black glass lit from behind. Like a night sky with sparkling stars.

I was puzzled. I tilted my head and looked at Mistress for an explanation.

She consulted the label below the display and read aloud, "The constellation *Canis Major* means *Big Dog*." She touched a glowing light. "See this star in the group of stars? It's the brightest star in the whole sky. People call it the Dog Star."

I want to hear more! If I keep wagging my tail ...

Mistress read further. "Its official name is Sirius. Beside it is the constellation *Orion*, the Great Hunter. Perhaps he and his dog are hunting

54

together through the night sky."

The clerk behind the counter, in a dark blue uniform with silver trim, grinned. He ran his fingertip across his moustache and bowed slightly.

"Gustavo," he said, touching his chest. "Welcome to the Hollywood Dog Star Hotel, Miss Schmoopie. Here, every guest is a star. We've been expecting you."

I stood taller while Mistress checked me in.

Gustavo shook my paw. "May I?"

He pressed my paw onto an inkpad before setting it firmly next to where Mistress had written my name. This left a clear impression of my right paw on the sign-in book. He scanned my microchip, too. *People take dogs seriously here!*

My jaw dropped at our suite. My room had a person-sized bed just for me. Special pillows decorated with paw prints looked comfy. Sunshine flooded in through a skylight. At night, if I woke up restless, I could watch the stars roll by. *Would I see the Dog Star?*

Mistress had her own separate room in the

SCHMOOPIE'S DREAM

suite. Whenever she was present we cuddled in the living-dining room or in her bed. During the day, while she took care of business at the movie studio, I had plenty to do.

A giant flat-screened TV filled the wall opposite my bed. *Bow-WOW!* During the first week, I watched many of the 500 movies starring dogs. The "valet" showed me how to operate the touch screen. I simply pressed the big square below the poster of any film I wanted to see. There was a dog-friendly TV channel, too.

I spent many happy hours watching Lassie rescue Timmy. I never got tired of her adventures. But I learned things from the other films. *Lady and the Tramp* is good for romantic daydreams. Except, in my case, I would have been the streetwise mutt. Maybe one day I'll meet a fellow of fancy breed ...

101 Dalmations is a horror film! Made my fur bristle. I wanted to sink my teeth into that evil woman in the black and white fur coat, trying to catch and skin puppies. That movie gave me nightmares.

Toto, Dorothy's little terrier in *The Wizard of Oz*, was very brave. Toto even challenged a lion! But those flying monkeys were terrible. Made me want to bite and shake them.

My special masseuse, Sophie, gave me a daily belly rub with scented oils. It was called Aromatherapy. Delicious. I'm glad to say Mistress never ordered the Blueberry Facial for me. Really!

Every day we had a busy activity schedule. No one was allowed to get plump! We had Guest Playtime on the roof to "meet and greet" buddies and romp over the designer constructions. The giant bone we raced through was my favorite. But the doghouse with three floors, slides for staircases, and swinging doors was fun, too.

We socialized in a gym area. Kind of like a cocktail hour. On the first day, I met three "guests" who were making films during their stay.

A dark German Shepherd came over. "Hello. I'm Bernard. Call me Bernie. I'm First Alternate in the remake of *Rin Tin Tin*. We have two days

SCHMOOPIE'S DREAM

off while they set up the next soundstage. What's your name?" We gave each other a good sniffing.

Wally, a hefty husky, said, "Hi, I'm playing Balto, the lead sled dog in the team that fought through a raging blizzard. A real-life hero. He led the final leg of a relay delivering influenza vaccine to save the children in Nome, Alaska, in 1925. Strong, like me. Who are you? What film are you making?"

"I'm Schmoopie. I'm just visiting," I said shyly. "But home in New York, there's a statue of Balto on our running route in Central Park." Wally was so big, I felt a bit intimidated. I sniffed him carefully.

And Muffy, a fluffy Bichon, was taping a pilot for a TV series about a dog-princess. "I can't reveal the name yet," she confided. "It's under development. Very hush-hush." We shared friendly nose rubs. I imagined possible names for the dog-princess: *Doggerella? Princess Cania?*

When Mistress had to work late, she arranged for a staff member to read me a bedtime story from the Hotel's huge library of dog-related books.

HOLLYWOOD DOG-STAR HOTEL

It's soothing to relax listening to a good story.

Having met Bernard, I loved hearing more adventures of *Rin Tin Tin*, a real German Shepherd in wartime. He was a sick puppy found by a serviceman and taken home to America where he grew strong. He became a big movie star and won the first dog Oscar. Hero-dogs are inspiring.

The Hotel had a webcam in each room so owners could check on their pets' well-being during any time of day or night. It was nice to know that if I had a problem, Mistress could see what was happening and get help.

The fancy bakery in the lobby was too rich for my taste, but some guests gobbled the éclairs and cupcakes made from dog-friendly ingredients. Then they needed more time in the gym.

The clothing boutique was also too much. Who wants a dog-purse or a matching outfit? Chihuahuas from Beverly Hills, maybe? *To each their favorite bone.*

Thank goodness Mistress doesn't dress me up. Except for Halloween. Last year, I was Yoda to her Darth Vader in black helmet and costume.

59

SCHMOOPIE'S DREAM

That was fun.

After four weeks of Playtime, endless dog-movies, dog-stories, massages and aromatherapy, I was ready to hit the road.

The celebrity groomer gave me a last brush, wash and blow-dry. My fur gleamed. When we had first arrived in Hollywood, Mistress telephoned to make an appointment at an upscale salon. They asked my breed. When Mistress revealed I was a mixed breed, the receptionist replied, "We do *not* groom mongrels."

Mistress was furious, and rightly so! Her tense stance and tight shoulders showed her anger. But she simply arranged private sessions at the Hotel from a celebrity groomer. She always keeps me looking fabulous.

Sean, who had stayed with relatives in Los Angeles, was to drive me back across the country. We had taken a Northern route coming to the West Coast. We would return by a Southern route.

I danced around, eager to start. Mistress would

Hollywood Dog-Star Hotel

fly home to Master. All of us would meet up at our Den on the East Coast.

Mistress's bags sat ready and waiting. I made a goodbye visit to the Playroom for quick sniffs and nose rubs.

Chapter 10
Cross Country Eastward

At the airport entrance, Mistress hugged me goodbye.

"Take care, Schmoopie. Have a fun, safe journey. See you in five days."

I licked her face.

"Love you!" She waved, blowing a kiss. I waved my tail. Homeward bound ...

Schmoopie's Dream

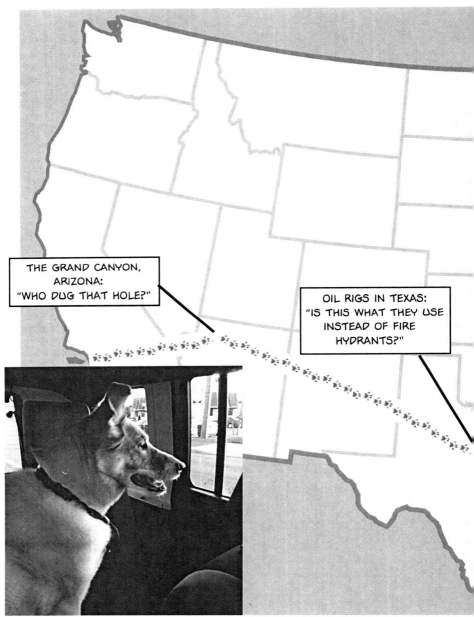

Cross Country Eastward

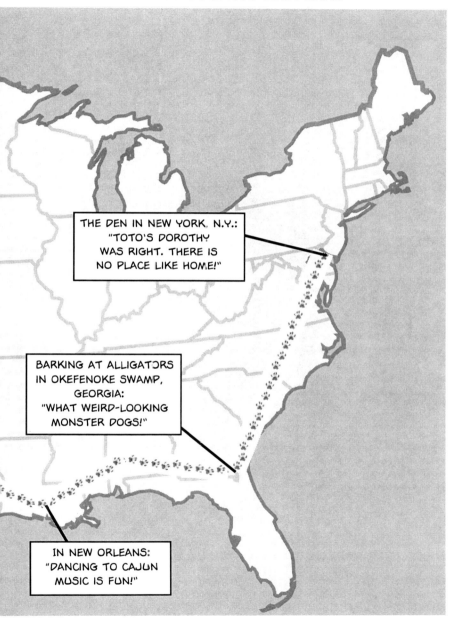

Chapter 11

Homecoming

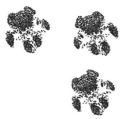

I stood on the deck of the yacht. Master needed Mistress below for a moment to check our schedule. I was safe alone. My life jacket was fastened and booties cushioned my paws.

The pale December 1st sun inched closer to the horizon. Reds and oranges fanned upward, lighting the scattered clouds like a fiery end-of-autumn tree. Streaks of golden light pierced through the last display as the sun set.

Our last yacht ride for months. Mistress should see how beautiful it is ...

Absorbed in admiring the setting sun, I ignored

SCHMOOPIE'S DREAM

the creak of a small rowboat that had pulled alongside the yacht.

Whomp! A fishing net flew over the side of the yacht.

Weights attached to the edges trapped me underneath the net, caught me like a breathless fish. I was too stunned to yelp.

Holy Dog Star!

One sniff of the man straddling the yacht's protective railing plunged me back to helpless puppyhood. *Oh, no! The bad man. Mean Mac.*

He clamped a muzzle around my jaws while the net ensnared me. It choked off the growl rising in my throat. He tightened and yanked the net, knocking me, big as I am, off my feet. He tugged me to the side of the deck.

I shook and tried to bite Mac, but the muzzle held tight. He lowered me, struggling, into another man's uplifted arms before jumping into the rowboat.

They're kidnapping me! Where will they take me?

Mac rowed swiftly to a big scruffy fishing boat. The two men clambered aboard, dragging me

68

HOMECOMING

after them.

Do they work for Cruella De Vil? Mistress! Master! HELP!

Mac secured the rowboat to the fishing boat, sat at the steering wheel, revved the motor and sped away.

I strained against the rope, half-choked, as the other man attached my collar to a ring on the side of the boat. I was in shock from the rough treatment But no bark escaped my muzzled mouth. The boat's motor drowned out the strangled noises in my throat.

Darkness settled over the harbor like a black blanket. Lights, like stars, blinked on in the vessels bobbing in the harbor. A single dim bulb lit the fishing boat. Hardly visible. In the apartment buildings bordering the harbor, windows lit up.

From the yacht, Mistress's voice rang out over the water, "Schmoopie? *Schmoopie!* Where are you?"

Silence. A flashlight moved slowly across the blackness. Master's deep voice shouted my name.

69

SCHMOOPIE'S DREAM

Muzzled, I could only tug against the rope that strangled me.

A Harbor Patrol police-boat swung dazzling searchlights back and forth over the inky water. *They're searching for me.* Floodlights passed across the fishing boat. *My master must have phoned his pal, the Harbormaster.*

"Joe, cut that life vest off the dog! And the collar. Get rid of any I.D. tags. Toss them overboard. Now!"

Joe did as his boss ordered. "Sorry, kiddo," he said softly.

Even through the muzzle, I smelled oil and mustard on Joe's hands. *Oh, it's the nice one.* I nudged him with my snout.

Joe stared. Sighed. "I can't do this," he murmured. He untied the rope that bound me to the boat and cut away the muzzle.

"Go, Girl," he whispered. "Quick as you can. Swim for your life!" He gave my rump a smack.

I shook myself and leapt over the edge into dark water.

70

HOMECOMING

Brr! Cold. Icy cold. I dog-paddled as if my tail were on fire.

Whistles pierced my ears.

"You in the fishing boat," one of the harbor policemen yelled. "Cut your engine."

"What's the problem, officer?" asked Mac, innocent-sounding.

"Have you seen a big dog? On any boat? Or in the water?"

"Nope. Nothing."

"Notify us if you do."

"Sure thing, Officer."

The Harbor Patrol motored slowly onward, its floodlight scanning the darkness.

I paddled desperately in the icy water. I'm strong, but not used to swimming. I shivered. The apartment buildings surrounding the harbor were too far to reach. Invisible in the shadow, I thrashed toward the police boat.

The Patrol motored slowly away. It turned in an arc and headed back in our direction.

"Joe, get rid of the dog!" Mac hissed back to his assistant.

71

SCHMOOPIE'S DREAM

"She jumped overboard, Mac."
"*What?* You idiot! Use the grappling hook. Quick. Throw one of the weights. *Sink it!*"
"No, Mac. I'm done! I'm finished with your dirty business."
"You're done all right! I'll do it myself." Mac set the motor on automatic. He rushed toward the back of the boat for the grappling hook. Joe blocked his way.
"No more."
Mac shoved Joe aside. Joe pushed back. Mac swung hard. Joe grabbed him with an iron grip. They locked together in a punching, smacking scuffle. Hardened fists slammed clenched jaws. A dogfight. Between men.
I pawed through the freezing water. I might make the Police boat, be pulled to safety. But the two men were fighting on the deck behind me. *Could I leave the kind man to chance? He saved me. Twice!*
Would Lassie swim away from danger? Would Rin Tin Tin desert? Would Toto leave Dorothy? I am as loyal as my dog heroes. I must help!

HOMECOMING

Something deep inside me welled up like a geyser. From the tip of my tail, up my wet spine it rose. A scream. Unstoppable. I threw back my head and howled. I pointed my nose to the Dog Star, rising bright on the horizon, and howled like my ancient ancestors. In the middle of the harbor, half drowned, dog paddling to save my life, I bellowed the age-old call to the Pack.

I howled for all the lonely dogs without a home. Howled for hungry dogs without someone to love them. Howled for dogs with cruel owners.

Every being within earshot shivered at the sound. People looked out windows. Turned on balcony lights. Called police. This was a city, not a forest or Arctic plain. There were no wolves left here.

But the Spirit of the Wolf arose in me and spread for six miles in every direction. I paddled in place and I bayed.

Inside the shabby fishing boat, where crates of skinny dogs were packed so tightly they could not stand or stretch their legs, the dogs heard me. And they answered.

73

SCHMOOPIE'S DREAM

In each cram-packed box in every corner of every crate, adult and puppy alike lifted their snouts and howled. The night air echoed with their cries.

"There!" shouted Master from the deck of his yacht. "Over there!" He pointed. The captain aimed for the sound.

The Harbor Patrol swung around. Floodlights blazed onto the deck of the fishing boat where two men were locked in conflict. The police patrol pulled closer.

"You there! *Freeze!* Harbor Police. We're coming aboard. Drop to the deck." A dozen searchlights converged on the shabby boat.

Mac froze in the blazing lights. Blinded, he shoved Joe to the deck. Kicked his back. Dove overboard on the dark side of the boat. I kept howling and the chorus yowled in reply.

A policeman yelled, "He's in the water!"

With strong strokes, Mac swam toward the closest dock.

He hauled himself onto a shadowy corner of the pier and slipped between stacks of crates ...

74

HOMECOMING

straight into the arms of Sean!

Whistles blew to signal to the rest of the patrol that the culprit was in custody.

I pictured an officer locking Mac into handcuffs and dragging him to the police van. He'd say, "Inside, you dirty dog! It's the doghouse for you for a long, long time."

When I saw a policeman on the fishing boat help the nice man stand up, I paddled back.

Arf! Arf!

They pulled me onto the deck. Mistress and Master boarded the fishing boat, too, from their yacht.

"Oh, Schmoopie! I thought we lost you!" Mistress sobbed and embraced me. She wrapped me in a fluffy white towel the policeman handed her, rubbing briskly to warm my chilled body.

"You were so brave! I'm proud of you."

"Good girl!" echoed Master with a sturdy pat. I twitched my wet tail.

Still draped in the thick towel, I plodded over to Joe where the police held him for questioning, licked his oily, mustard-scented hands. Mistress

SCHMOOPIE'S DREAM

and Master stared. Astonished.

"The mutt and I go way back," Joe explained with a smile on his bruised face. He rubbed my head. "She's such a sweet pooch, I left her at the Humane Society a year-and-a-half ago. She's so loving, I thought she deserved a chance to be loved."

Mistress and Master exchanged looks.

"There's something you should see," Joe said. He led the group inside the hull to the sealed crates, alive with whimpers and weak barks. Policemen pried open the crates.

I stared at the sickly litter. I had been one of these poor creatures. Mama Dog and my brothers and sisters had been, too. I nuzzled the nearest pups.

Master and the police captain huddled. As leader of our Den, Master suggested a solution. The sickly dogs had to undergo quarantine. But when the period was over, those that were cleared as healthy would be turned over to him and Mistress.

HOMECOMING

During the forty-day quarantine period, Mistress found and bought an airy building near the Beach House. She had it cleaned and equipped with the best amenities of the Hollywood Dog-Star Hotel: a playroom, a gym, running space, a wading pool, massage areas, books and movies about dogs.

She even had a small theater installed for dog actors to perform in plays. *Maybe my friends from Hollywood can act in them ...*

In large print, a brass plate on the front of the house reads:

Schmoopie's Haven for Homeless Dogs

The first time I saw the brass plate, I lifted my snout and loosed a happy howl. *It was worth everything!*

Chapter 12

Afterword

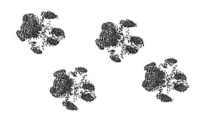

As a repeat offender, Mac received a prison sentence of five years for operating an illegal puppy mill. The judge warned Joe to never get involved in illegal activity again. For his help in saving the pups, his sentence was reduced to 400 hours of community service. He was allowed to work it off at *Schmoopie's Haven.*

After he completed his sentence, Mistress hired Joe as Top Dog. Joe brought in Bright Eyes from the Humane Society to help him find and supervise kindly caretakers and dog trainers.

He appointed himself driver of the Haven

Schmoopie's Dream

Rescue Van. Sometimes I sit beside Joe on rescue missions. *Like a police dog!*

In a ceremony at City Hall, I received a special honorary award for bravery. The mayor placed the ribbon with the medal around my neck. Mistress, Master, Sean, Brian, Joe and Bright Eyes clapped. I felt as grand as Lassie, Rin Tin Tin, and Toto put together. I had earned my V.I.D. (Very Important Dog) Award: *Bravery knows no breed.*

After the Haven was running smoothly, Joe and Bright Eyes, whose name turned out to be Brianna, married. Of course, Master and Mistress attended their wedding, held on the beach in front of their Beach House. I carried a basket of pink rose petals down the sandy aisle. I watched the ceremony with wagging tail.

AFTERWORD

Mistress's tummy grew large. One day I gazed into the blue eyes of a beautiful baby boy. My own special charge. I spread my loyalty to include the new member of the Den. I stretched it wider to include a second baby boy. By then, the first boy was my close friend and playmate.

Once a week Mistress, the boys, and I visit *Schmoopie's Haven for Homeless Dogs* to meet new friends. We attend an occasional play in *Schmoopie's Dog-Star Theater.* On opening night, my Hollywood friend Fluffy starred as the Princess in *Doggerella.*

Back at the Beach House, we play. I romp in the surf, snap at the waves and dig up treasures. I pick the shiniest, prettiest shell and carry it to the blanket where Mistress rests, cradling the baby. I drop my gift in front of Mistress, my Lady Alpha.

"Thank you Schmoopie!" Mistress says. She rubs me in my favorite spots. Behind the ears. Under the chin. Between the brows on my velvety diamond.

When I'm worn out with play, I lie down on the blanket beside them. Dog-tired, I sleep.

SCHMOOPIE'S DREAM

*I knead the air with my paws.
I suck.
My closed eyes dart back and forth.
My tail thuds.
Whistles puff my lips.
They are back with me,
Mama Dog and my brothers and sisters ...*

... this time when I wake up, I am not alone. My new family is there beside me. Warm. Cozy. Mistress's arm rests on my neck. The boy nestles against my back. The baby's pudgy hand pets my fur. Master waves from the surf.
    My tail flip-flops with joy.

Listen Up!

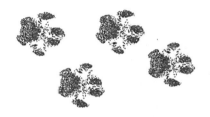

A Short List of Good Films Featuring Dogs

A Few Facts about the Dog Star

A Few Facts about Dogs

SCHMOOPIE'S DREAM

Listen Up!

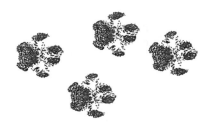

A Short List of Good Films Featuring Dogs

1. The Wizard of Oz (1939)
Dorothy Gale, who lives on a farm with her Auntie Em and Uncle Henry, runs away from home with her dog, Toto. Caught by a tornado, she returns home, is struck on the head, and falls into bed as the house is lifted by the tornado. She "awakens" in a magical land where she befriends the Scarecrow, the Tin Man, and the Cowardly Lion. They embark on a quest down

SCHMOOPIE'S DREAM

the Yellow Brick Road to consult the Great Wizard of Oz, from whom each one hopes to get their heart's desire.

After defeating the Wicked Witch of the West, and helped by Glinda the Good Witch of the North, and the Ruby Slippers, they succeed. The Scarecrow gets a brain, The Tin Man a heart, and the Lion a medal for Bravery; Dorothy is able to return home.

One of the great films of all time, this classic won the year's Best Musical Score, Best Song (for "Over the Rainbow"), and a Special Junior Oscar for Judy Garland as Dorothy. L. F. Baum wrote the novel on which the movie is based.

2. Lassie Come Home (1943)

A poor family is forced to sell the family dog, a collie named Lassie. She escapes from her new owner and makes the difficult journey from Scotland back to the home of her heart in Yorkshire, England. Classic. Many versions exist. This one, starring Roddy McDowell and Elizabeth Taylor as children, is one of the best.

LISTEN UP!

3. Lady and the Tramp (1955)

A romance develops between a Cocker Spaniel from a fancy uptown home and a streetwise Mutt from downtown. Walt Disney. Nominated for a Bafta award.

4. A Dog of Flanders (1991)

A poor boy in Belgium, Nello, is an orphan who lives with his grandfather. He finds a dog almost beaten to death and names it Patrasche. Well cared for, Patrasche (a *Bouvier de Flandres* dog) survives and he and the boy become inseparable. Nello helps his grandfather sell milk with Patrasche pulling the cart. The boy falls in love with a rich girl who admires his drawings. Together, Nello and his dog face many adventures and dangers. Eventually, Nello is recognized as a great artist.

Based on an 1872 novel by Marie Louise de la Ramée, under her penname, Ouida. A statue of Nello and Patrasche stands in the Antwerp suburb of Hoboken, Belgium. Several Japanese versions of the film exist.

89

SCHMOOPIE'S DREAM

5. 101 Dalmations (1996)

The wealthy owner of a house of fashion design in London, Cruella de Vil, has her henchmen kidnap litters of Dalmation puppies to kill them for their spotted fur, planning to make herself a special coat from their skins. Several animals cooperate to outwit the henchmen and defeat Cruella. Based on the novel by Dodie Smith.

6. Beverly Hills Chihuahua (2008)

Chloe, a rich, elegant Chihuahua from Beverly Hills, gets lost while on vacation in Mexico. She needs the help of fellow dogs to escape dangers and return home.

7. Up (2009)

Carl, a 78-year-old widower, tries to fulfill his lifelong dream to see Paradise Falls in South America by tying thousands of balloons to his old house. An eight-year-old wilderness explorer, Russell, and a stray dog, called Dug, become stowaways when the house is airborne. Many adventures follow.

LISTEN UP!

Pixar Animation Studios and Walt Disney Pictures. This film received five Academy Award nominations, including a nomination for Best Picture. It received great critical acclaim and was a huge financial success.

8. Hachi (2009)

Based on the true story of an abandoned puppy (an *Akita Inu*) taken home by a college professor. Hachi sees his master off at the train station every morning and awaits his return every evening. When Professor Wilson dies of a heart attack at work one day, his faithful dog waits for him to return every evening for the next nine years, until his own death.

This film is sad but also is an inspiring and uplifting depiction of loyalty.

A statue of Hachi exists in the very spot, in front of the train station in Shibuya, Japan where he waited for his master.

SCHMOOPIE'S DREAM

A Few Facts About the Dog Star

Some people say that the constellation named Big Dog (officially called Canis Major because Canis means "dog" and Major means "big" in Latin) looks like a dog barking at Orion the hunter. Early astronomers pictured the Big Dog as Orion's hunting partner. Other myths say the Big Dog is Laelaps, the fastest and favorite hunting dog of Diana, goddess of the hunt.

Depending on how the Big Dog is visualized connecting the stars in the group, the brightest star, Sirius, seems to be in the dog's chest or, if only the head is pictured, on the dog's forehead. Sirius is actually composed of two overlapping stars (a binary star).

Sirius seems to be the brightest star in the sky (anything brighter is a planet) because it is closer to earth than other stars. The rising of Sirius in the eastern sky just before sunrise signaled for Ancient Egyptians that it was time for the annual flooding of the Nile. The rising waters fertilized and softened the soil, preparing it for the next

LISTEN UP!

crop. The rising of the Nile always occurred in the heat of late July or August, which became known as the "Dog Days."

Orion is one of the brightest constellations. He is easy to spot when he is in the night sky because of the three bright stars forming his belt. The brilliant star called Betelgeuse (pronounced BEETLE-juice) is on Orion's shoulder. The word Betegeuse is Arabic for "shoulder of the giant." Another bright star, named Rigel (RYE-gel), appears on Orion's right knee.

The constellation of the Big Dog is located to the left of Orion's left knee, as if he is accompanying his master on the hunt.

A Few Facts about Dogs

Dogs dream. just as most mammals do (with the exception of the spiny anteater). You can sometimes watch dogs dream; their eyes move back and forth under closed lids; their legs often twitch and move as if running.

Dogs see mainly in shades of gray. Blue, how-

SCHMOOPIE'S DREAM

ever, is a vivid color for dogs. Perhaps blue was selected through evolution as an aid to finding water. Vision in dogs is not as keen as it is for people.

Dogs' sense of smell is at least 1,000 times more sensitive than in humans. They have 20 to 25 times more smell receptors than people do. Dogs' long noses are well adapted to help them remember with their noses.

Dogs also hear much better than people. They can perceive high-pitched sounds that people cannot hear. Their keen hearing and sense of smell make them useful helpers for the police.

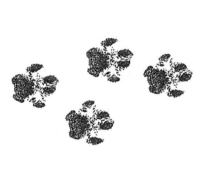

Schmoopie's Dream

About the Author

Patricia Garfield is a renowned expert in dreams; her Ph.D. is in Clinical Psychology. Author of twelve books on dreams, Patricia's bestseller *Creative Dreaming* (1974, 1995) is considered a classic and appears in fifteen languages. She won the 2002 Parents' Guide Media Award for *The Dream Book*. In 2012, The International Association for the Study of Dreams granted her an award for *Lifetime Achievement in Dreamwork*. Her website *www.creativedreaming.org* draws visitors from around the globe.

Patricia has recorded her own dreams for more than 65 years.

She thanks Schmoopie's family for sharing their photographs of her and some of the stories of her adventures for this True Pet Tail. Other stories about Schmoopie originated in the author's imagination.

Authenticated by Schmoopie

CPSIA information can be obtained
at www.ICGtesting.com
Printed in the USA
FFOW01n1952090714
6299FF